Going to the Dentist

by Helen Frost

Consulting Editor:
Gail Saunders-Smith, Ph.D.

Consultant:
Karen Masbaum Yoder, RDH, Ph.D.
Indiana University
School of Dentistry

Pebble Books

an imprint of Capstone Press
Mankato, Minnesota

Pebble Books are published by Capstone Press
818 North Willow Street, Mankato, Minnesota 56001
http://www.capstone-press.com

Library of Congress Cataloging-in-Publication Data
Frost, Helen, 1949–
    Going to the dentist/by Helen Frost.
    p. cm.—(Dental health)
    Includes bibliographical references and index.
    Summary: An introductory look at a dentist's office, including the equipment
found there, what the dentist does during a check-up, and cavities.
    ISBN 0-7368-0114-6
    1. Dentistry—Juvenile literature. 2. Children—Preparation for dental care—
Juvenile literature. [1. Dental care. 2. Dentistry.] I. Title. II. Series: Frost, Helen, 1949–
Dental health.
    RK63.F755 1999
    617.6—dc21   98-7176
                                                                            CIP
                                                                            AC

Note to Parents and Teachers

This series supports the health education standards for how to
maintain personal health. This book describes a dentist's office and
what happens during a visit to the dentist. The photographs support
emergent readers in understanding the text. Repetition of words and
phrases helps emergent readers learn new words. This book
introduces emergent readers to vocabulary used in this subject area.
The vocabulary is defined in the Words to Know section. Emergent
readers may need assistance in reading some words and in using the
Table of Contents, Words to Know, Read More, Internet Sites, and
Index/Word List sections of the book.

2

Table of Contents

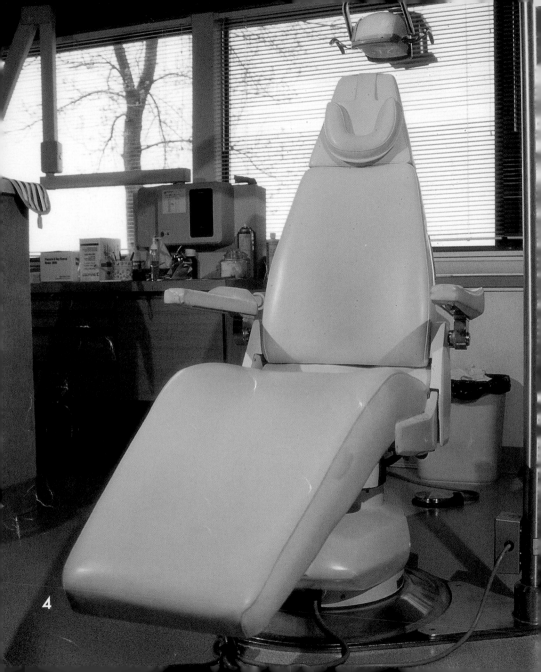

4

The dentist's office has a big chair. The chair moves up and down.

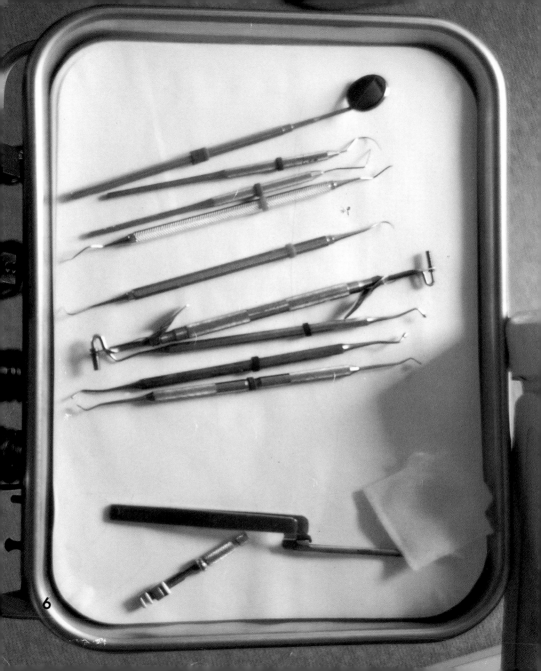

The dentist's office has a tray. The tray holds the dentist's tools.

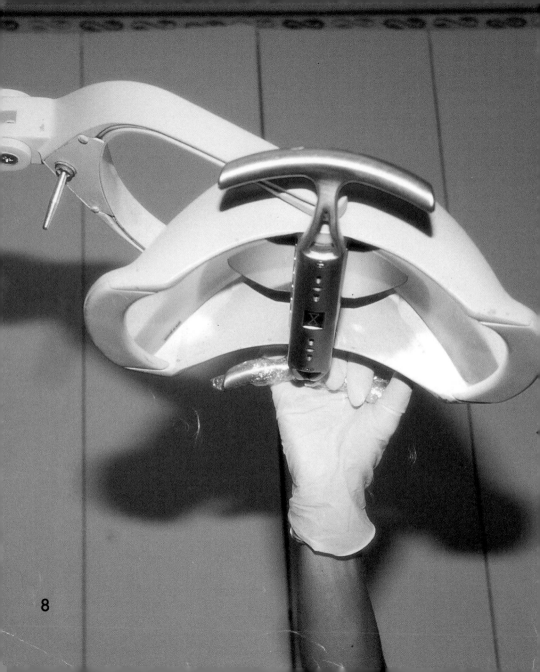

8

The dentist's office has a
bright light. The light
helps the dentist see
inside people's mouths.

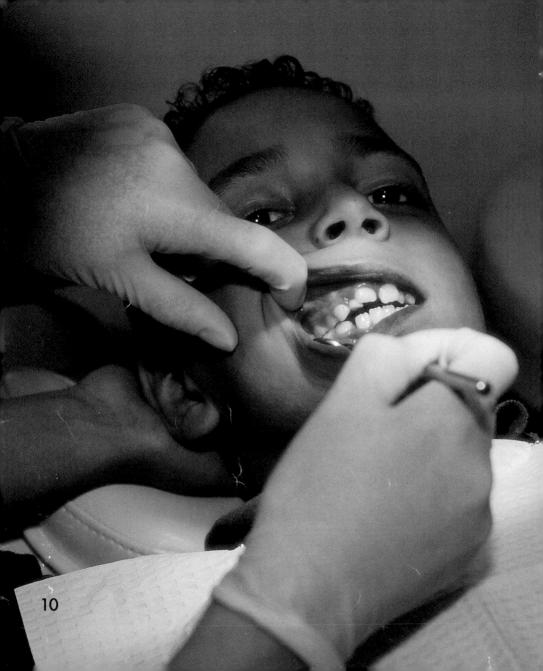

The dentist looks at people's teeth and gums.

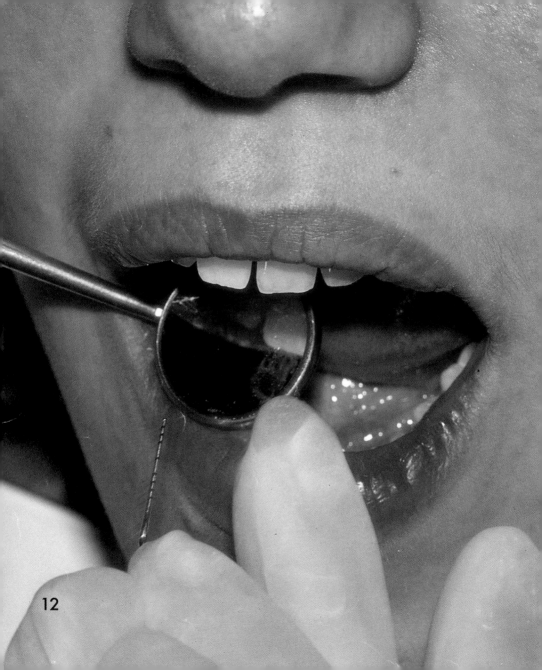

12

The dentist uses a mouth mirror. The mouth mirror shows the backs of teeth.

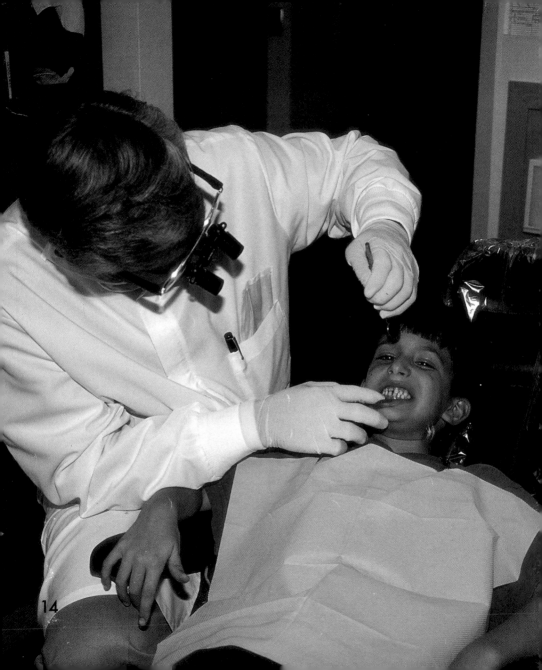

The dentist checks to see if teeth are growing straight.

The dentist looks for cavities. A cavity is a decayed part of a tooth.

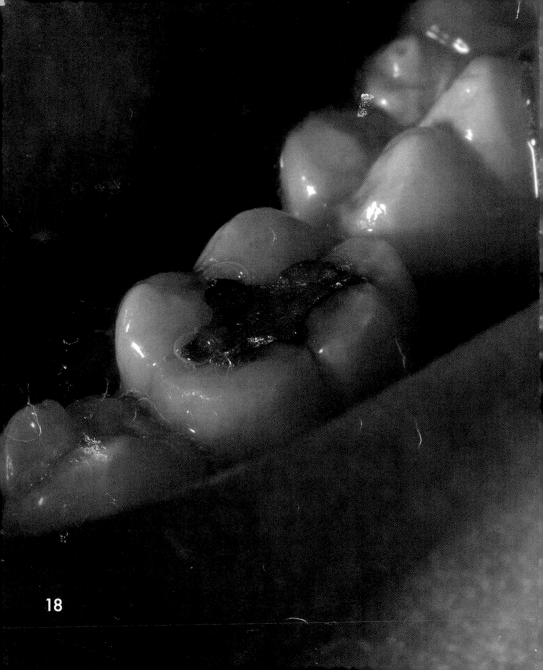

18

The dentist fixes cavities so they do not get bigger. The dentist takes out the decayed part. The dentist puts in a filling.

Sometimes the dentist finds only healthy teeth. That makes the dentist happy.

Words to Know

cavity—a decayed part of a tooth; a dentist takes out the decayed part and puts in a filling.

decayed—broken down; people can avoid tooth decay by brushing their teeth after they eat.

dentist—a person who knows how to check, clean, and fix teeth

filling—matter put into a tooth to stop decay

gums—the firm, pink skin around the base of teeth

mouth mirror—a tiny, round mirror with a long handle; dentists use mouth mirrors to see the backs of teeth.

straight—not bent; teeth that do not grow straight might not work right.

Read More

Chambliss, Maxie. *I'm Going to the Dentist.* New York: Ladybird Books, 1997.

Gillis, Jennifer Storey. *Tooth Truth: Fun Facts and Projects.* Pownal, Vt.: Storey Communications, 1996.

Hallinan, P.K. *My Dentist, My Friend.* Nashville, Tenn.: Ideals Children's Books, 1996.

Internet Sites

American Dental Association Kids' Corner
http://www.ada.org/consumer/kids/index.html

The Pediatric Dentist
http://www.aapd.org/PedDent.html

Your Child's First Visit to the Dentist
http://www.ada.org/consumer/ncdhm/dudley01.html

Index/Word List

Word Count: 122
Early-Intervention Level: 7

Editorial Credits
Colleen Sexton, editor; Clay Schotzko/Icon Productions, cover designer; Sheri Gosewisch, photo researcher

Photo Credits
David F. Clobes, 4, 10, 18, 20
Images International/Ronald Cantor, 14
Kevin Vandivier, 16
Maguire PhotograFX/Joseph P. Maguire, 6
Thomas D. Parker, 8
Uniphoto/Daemmrich, cover
Visuals Unlimited/Eric Anderson, 1; Bill Beatty, 12